National Strategy for Aviation Security

March 26, 2007

The National Strategy for Aviation Security

Prologue

The security and economic prosperity of the United States depend significantly upon the secure operation of its aviation system and use of the world's airspace by the Nation, its international partners, and legitimate commercial interests. Terrorists, criminals, and hostile nation-states have long viewed aviation as a target for attack and exploitation. The tragic events of September 11, 2001 and the Heathrow plot of August 2006 are telling reminders of the threats facing aviation and the intent and capabilities of adversaries that mean to do harm to the United States and its people.

In June 2006, building upon the Administration's successful efforts since 9/11, the President directed the development of a comprehensive National Strategy for Aviation Security (hereafter referred to as "the Strategy") to protect the Nation and its interests from threats in the Air Domain.[1] The Secretary of Homeland Security, in accordance with National Security Presidential Directive-47/Homeland Security Presidential Directive-16 (NSPD-47/HSPD-16), will coordinate the operational implementation of the Strategy, including the integration and synchronization of related Federal programs and initiatives.

Aviation security is best achieved by integrating public and private aviation security global activities into a coordinated effort to detect, deter, prevent, and defeat threats to the Air Domain, reduce vulnerabilities, and minimize the consequences of, and expedite the recovery from, attacks that might occur. The Strategy aligns Federal government aviation security programs and initiatives into a comprehensive and cohesive national effort involving appropriate Federal, State, local, and tribal governments and the private sector to provide active layered aviation security for, and support defense in-depth of, the United States.

Through a collaborative interagency effort and with input from aviation stakeholders, seven supporting plans will be developed to address the specific threats and challenges identified in NSPD-47/HSPD-16. Although the plans will address different aspects of aviation security, they will be mutually linked and reinforce each other. The supporting plans are:

- Aviation Transportation System Security Plan;
- Aviation Operational Threat Response Plan;
- Aviation Transportation System Recovery Plan;
- Air Domain Surveillance and Intelligence Integration Plan;
- International Aviation Threat Reduction Plan;
- Domestic Outreach Plan; and
- International Outreach Plan.

Development of these plans will be guided by the need to revalidate and further enhance current aviation security principles. These plans will be updated on a periodic basis in response to

---

[1] Air Domain is defined as the global airspace, including domestic, international, and foreign airspace, as well as all manned and unmanned aircraft operating, and people and cargo present in that airspace, and all aviation-related infrastructures.

changes in perceived risks to aviation security, the world environment, technology, air transport demands, the global aviation system, and national and homeland security policies. Together, the Strategy and seven supporting plans present a comprehensive national effort to prevent hostile or illegal acts within the Air Domain, promote global economic stability, and protect legitimate aviation activities.

Introduction

"America historically has relied heavily on two vast oceans and two friendly neighbors for border security, and on the private sector for most forms of domestic transportation security. The increasing mobility and destructive potential of modern terrorism has required the United States to rethink and renovate fundamentally its systems for border and transportation security. Indeed, we must now begin to conceive of border security and transportation security as fully integrated requirements because our domestic transportation systems are inextricably intertwined with the global transport infrastructure. Virtually every community in America is connected to the global transportation network by the seaports, airports, highways, pipelines, railroads, and waterways that move people and goods into, within, and out of the Nation. We must therefore promote the efficient and reliable flow of people, goods, and services across borders, while preventing terrorists from using transportation conveyances or systems to deliver implements of destruction."

National Strategy for Homeland Security

The United States has a vital national interest in protecting its people, infrastructure, and other interests from threats in the Air Domain. The differences between ground-based and airborne aviation security measures implemented in different jurisdictions throughout the world, the volume of domestic and international air traffic, the speed with which events unfold, and the complexity of aviation assets make the Air Domain uniquely susceptible to attack or exploitation by terrorist groups, hostile nation-states, and criminals.

Adversaries have demonstrated the ability and a continuing desire to exploit vulnerabilities and to adapt to changes in aviation security measures by conducting multiple, simultaneous, catastrophic attacks against the United States and its global interests. Exploitation of the Air Domain by terrorists and hostile nation-states using unconventional attack methods is not a recent phenomenon. In the 1970s, overseas militant groups hijacked commercial passenger aircraft as a means of garnering international media attention to further their causes. The rise of Islamic religious extremism and state-sponsored terrorism spawned further attacks against civil aviation, including: the hijacking of Trans World Airlines Flight 847 in 1985; the hijacking of Pan Am Flight 73 in 1986 in Karachi, Pakistan; the destruction of Pan Am Flight 103 over Scotland in 1988; and the downing of a French UTA aircraft over Niger in 1989. The attacks of September 11, 2001, brought the reality of these methods to the United States; the Heathrow plot of August 2006 reminds us of the continuing danger.

Over the past five years, the security of the aviation sector has been significantly strengthened through the efforts of the Federal government working with State, local, and tribal governments, the international community, and the private sector. Together these partners continue to implement a broad range of aviation security measures through innovative initiatives and by leveraging pre-existing capabilities to provide the Nation with an active, layered aviation security, and defense in-depth. Such measures include: a federalized Transportation Security Officer workforce that screens passengers and baggage traveling on passenger aircraft; hardened cockpit doors to prevent unauthorized access to the flight deck; Federal Air Marshals who fly anonymously on commercial passenger aircraft to provide a law enforcement presence; enhanced explosives and threat detection technology deployed in hundreds of airports; airspace and air traffic management security measures; and a cadre of canine explosives detection teams screening baggage, cargo, and increasingly, carry-on items.

Other important security activities include: thousands of pilots who voluntarily participate in the Federal Flight Deck Officer program, which permits trained pilots to carry firearms; flight crew members, including flight attendants who have voluntarily taken the Transportation Security Administration's (TSA) Advanced Flight Crew Self-Defense course; other Federal, State, local, and tribal law enforcement officers who travel armed as part of their normal duties; establishment of a program to collect and analyze suspicious events; efforts to streamline operational coordination on incidents both in the air and on the ground; daily vetting of thousands of crew members and passengers on flights to and from the United States; and improvement of surveillance and intelligence sharing. In addition, the Nation's air defense mission has been transformed by expanding surveillance and air interdiction efforts inward to counter terrorist air threats, as well as by continuing traditional air defense activities against the threats from hostile nation-states.

In today's global and interconnected economy, the safe movement of people and cargo across the open skies is a crucial factor in promoting free trade and advancing prosperity and freedom. Defeating the array of threats to the Air Domain requires a common understanding of, and a coordinated effort for, action on a global scale. Nations have a common interest to protect global air travel. Since all nations benefit from this collective security, the United States must encourage all nations to share the responsibility for maintaining aviation security by countering the threats in this domain.

The Aviation Transportation System[2] comprises a broad spectrum of private and public sector elements, including: aircraft and airport operators; over 19,800 private and public use airports; the aviation sector; and a dynamic system of facilities, equipment, services, and airspace. The Aviation Transportation System continues to grow rapidly, as more and more passengers regularly choose to fly. On a daily basis, thousands of carrier flights arrive, depart, or overfly the continental United States, while each year millions of tons of freight and thousands of tons of mail are transported by air in the United States.

The Nation must be capable of stopping terrorist groups, hostile nation-states, and criminals before they can threaten or engage in attacks against the United States and its international partners, including through the use of weapons of mass destruction (WMD). To achieve these ends, Federal, State, local, and tribal governments and the private sector must take full advantage of strengthened intelligence collection, analysis, and appropriate dissemination; increased sharing of surveillance and other aviation resources; advances in technology; continued enhancements in aviation protective measures; innovations in the use of law enforcement personnel; and strengthened alliances within the public and private sector and other international cooperative arrangements. Military air defense assets are integrated into those activities to provide seamless coverage.

---

[2] The Aviation Transportation System is defined as U.S. airspace, all manned and unmanned aircraft operating in that airspace, all U.S. aviation operators, airports, airfields, air navigation services, and related infrastructure, and all aviation-related industry.

The Strategy does not alter existing authorities or responsibilities of department and agency heads, including their authorities to carry out operational activities or to provide or receive information. It does not change or otherwise affect the authority of the Secretary of Defense over the Department of Defense, including the chain of command for military forces from the President, to the Secretary of Defense, to the military commanders or military command and control procedures.

Three broad principles provide overarching guidance to the Strategy, its objectives, and its actions. First, the Nation must use the full range of its assets and capabilities to prevent the Air Domain from being exploited by terrorist groups, hostile nation-states, and criminals to commit acts against the United States, its people, its infrastructure, and its other interests. Second, the Nation must ensure the safe and efficient use of the Air Domain. Third, the Nation must continue to facilitate travel and commerce. These guiding principles are critical to global stability and economic growth and are vital to the interests of the United States.

Threats to the Air Domain

Threats to the Air Domain are numerous, complex, and adaptive. While conventional military threats in the Air Domain continue and will likely increase in times of international tension or conflict, the greatest current threat, as demonstrated in the Heathrow plot of August 2006 reminds us of the continuing danger, and therefore the focus of the Strategy, is terrorism.

Globalization, technological advances, the proliferation of WMD, and the emergence of terrorism as a global phenomenon have enabled threats to the Air Domain to extend in reach, accelerate in speed, and increase in potential impact. Aviation is a global enterprise with a distributed infrastructure and multiple access points. Successful attacks in the Air Domain can inflict mass casualties and grave economic damage, and attract significant public attention because of the impact on the modern transportation system.

Intelligence on threats to the Air Domain plays a critical role in assessing terrorist groups' intentions and capabilities and requires regular update and review to ensure that Federal, State, local, and tribal governments, the private sector, and the international community are taking appropriate measures. However, even the best intelligence will not uncover every specific terrorist plot because of terrorists' efforts at operational secrecy.

Threats focused on the Air Domain can be analyzed in two ways: by originator and by targets and tactics.

Threat Originators

There are three main originators of threats: terrorist groups; hostile nation-states; and other criminals.

Terrorist Groups. Terrorist groups are politically, as well as religiously in some cases, motivated and use premeditated violence, usually against noncombatants, to affect a particular audience. Because of their clear intent to do harm to the United States and its interests, terrorist groups remain the most severe threat to America's security. Their ultimate goal in the Air Domain is to conduct multiple, simultaneous, catastrophic attacks exploiting the Aviation Transportation System because of its visibility as a symbol of the U.S. global presence and economic influence. In addition, the attacks of September 11, 2001, and other successful or attempted attacks have inspired emulation.

The terrorist threat is changing in form and intensity as terrorists' intentions and capabilities change and countermeasures are instituted. Their techniques are adapting on multiple fronts, including modality of planning, complexity of attack, and style of execution. The type, location, and frequency of terrorist attacks cannot be reliably extrapolated from historical patterns, and therefore current threats must be regularly reassessed.

Terrorist groups, best typified by al-Qa'ida and its affiliates, pose several threats to the Air Domain. The most prominent threat is physical attack, discussed at greater length in the Targets and Tactics section of the Strategy. Terrorists might also take advantage of the same tactics, techniques, and methods pioneered by criminals to counter immigration, customs, and border security measures to move people and materiel. They might deploy in regions of political and economic instability where aviation law enforcement is stretched thin or readily corruptible, bribe officials, use forged fraudulent documents, and make illegal transactions to hide their true intentions. Terrorists might use unsecured air transportation routes to transport arms, explosives, or operatives clandestinely to safe havens, training sites, or attack-staging locations. Ultimately, terrorists might use these access points and routes to transport more dangerous cargo, including WMD and their associated components. Such threats are particularly worrisome in areas where governments are weak or provide safe haven to terrorists.

Hostile Nation-States. While most countries have an explicit interest in being able to operate safely, effectively, and reliably in the Air Domain, some pose threats, either due to actual hostile intent or weak infrastructure safeguards. For example, some countries directly sponsor international terrorism, providing training, funding, supplies, WMD and related components, and operational direction to surrogates. Other nation-states knowingly or unknowingly provide safe havens for terrorists who plan, prepare, or facilitate attacks or deploy materiel or operatives through the Air Domain. Some states have weak command and control over their aviation infrastructure, such as their internal air defenses or airport security apparatus, which terrorists can then exploit. Additionally, nation-states could present a military threat, such as cruise missiles, to the United States and U.S. interests globally in the Air Domain.

Criminals. Criminals, including individuals and groups, use the Air Domain to pursue objectives that are illegal under U.S. law or international convention. Domestic extremists in the United States have not, to date, engaged in organized efforts to attack the Aviation Transportation System. However, there are potentially violent domestic groups and individuals who have extensive knowledge of the aviation sector coupled with a demonstrated expertise in manufacturing and employing targeted-attack techniques, including improvised or conventional explosive devices.

Targets and Tactics

There are three primary categories of threats: to and from aircraft; to the Aviation Transportation System infrastructure; and from hostile exploitation of cargo.

Threats to and from Aircraft. Aircraft can be disaggregated into four categories of threats:
- large passenger aircraft;
- large all-cargo aircraft;
- small aircraft, such as aircraft used primarily to transport small numbers of people or to provide unique services, including light private and corporate aircraft, and helicopters; and
- non-traditional aircraft, such as unmanned aerial vehicles (UAVs), ultra-light aircraft, gliders, and aerial-application aircraft.

These categories might be susceptible to, or could pose a threat from, similar basic tactics: explosives; stand-off weapons including man-portable air defense systems (MANPADS); hijackings; WMD delivery and dissemination; and smuggling of terrorists and instruments of terror.

Large passenger aircraft. Historically, large passenger aircraft have been at the greatest risk to terrorism because terrorists perceive that such aircraft have great potential to inflict catastrophic damage and are likely to disrupt the Aviation Transportation System. Two tactics have appeared to date. First, aircraft and passengers have been used as targets, such as the detonation of a bomb onboard – as was central to the Heathrow plot of 2006, the taking of hostages, traditional hijacking, and attack from stand-off weapons including MANPADS. Second, aircraft have been used as weapons, most notably seen during the September 11, 2001, attacks. The Nation must closely monitor other tactics as they emerge.

Large all-cargo aircraft. Absent more attractive targets, such as large passenger aircraft, terrorists might seek to take advantage of the varying degrees and sophistication of security measures employed for all-cargo aircraft. If terrorist tactics adapt in this way, large all-cargo aircraft are likely more attractive as weapons, such as through a hijacking to attack ground-based targets or as conveyance mechanisms, rather than as targets. These aircraft also remain at risk from attacks using MANPADS or other stand-off weapons.

Small aircraft. As with large passenger aircraft, small aircraft face two varieties of threats: as the target of attack; or as weapons used to attack other targets. Small aircraft are relatively unattractive as targets because they carry few passengers, and thus would have less dramatic impact if attacked. As weapons, however, there are several potential threat scenarios. Terrorists might use a wide range of small aircraft, such as business jets or helicopters, to destroy a critical asset or portion of infrastructure. The most serious threat stems from terrorists using small aircraft to transport or deliver WMD or related materiel. The Nation must be especially watchful for terrorists adopting this tactic. Transnational criminal elements employ small aircraft to conduct illicit activities in the Air Domain, including smuggling of persons and contraband.

Non-traditional aircraft. While ultra-lights, remote-controlled aircraft, gliders, aerial-application aircraft, and UAVs have limited potential as targets, terrorists might employ these non-traditional aircraft as weapons or as a means to disseminate WMD. For example, terrorists might use them for missions that are of limited range, require limited accuracy, and have a specific and small target. Adoption of this tactic deserves very close monitoring.

While attacks against the Air Domain and the United States and its interests are currently more likely to originate from terrorists, the threat posed by military aircraft of hostile nation-states, such as long range strategic aviation, air-to-air missiles, long-range air-to-surface missiles, or cruise missiles must be considered.

Threats to the Aviation Transportation System Infrastructure. Reported threats to Aviation Transportation System infrastructure, which comprises airports and those facilities and systems that are used to provide Air Navigation Services (ANS) and other important related services needed to support air operations in U.S. airspace, are relatively few. In part, this is due to the relatively low public profile of ANS infrastructure such as Air Traffic Control facilities and systems, the robustness and resilience of these systems due to many layers of redundancies, and the Nation's likely capacity to recover rapidly and thus limit the psychological or economic impact of any attack.

There is a range of potential threat scenarios at different types of airport facilities that require vigilance. Terrorists might target passenger concentrations at commercial airports, recycling tactics from many years ago. They might place explosives near or inside passenger facilities. Terrorists might target multi-use airports, such as those combining commercial and military operations or commercial and general aviation operations, where unrelated security authorities and dissimilar security procedures often co-exist.

Other Aviation Transportation System-related threats are less likely to materialize. For example, general aviation airports have relatively few passengers in transit and an attack on one would present limited opportunities for causing major symbolic or economic damage. In addition, facilities that process high volumes of cargo have great redundancy and involve few people relative to the commercial passenger aviation system.

Threats from Hostile Exploitation of Cargo. The air-cargo industry is highly dynamic and encompasses a wide range of users, making it subject to potential exploitation by terrorists. Many users are regulated, from large all-cargo carriers, such as express consignment carriers that operate complex sorting operations at major hubs for time-definite cargo delivery, to small regional carriers, such as those that move high-value cargo or service rural areas. Since the adoption of enhanced security measures at airfreight terminals following September 11, 2001, threats such as stowaways aboard air freighters and the use of explosives for detonation have waned. However, the regulatory framework for cargo systems is not immune to exploitation, especially to methods that have been used by criminals for years. For example, terrorists may infiltrate the cargo handling system to transport people, conventional or WMD, or weapon components.

Risk Methodology

The Strategy will use a risk-based, cross-discipline, and global approach to aviation security to ensure that resources are allocated to those Federal, State, local, and tribal governments and private sector aviation security efforts with the greatest potential to prevent, detect, deter, and defeat attacks, and to mitigate the consequences if an attack occurs. The risk methodology used is outlined in the National Infrastructure Protection Plan (NIPP) and defined in more detail by the NIPP Transportation Sector-Specific Plan (TSSP). These plans define risk as a function of threat, vulnerability, and consequence. The United States Government will regularly conduct formal assessments of the risks to the Aviation Transportation System.

Strategic Objectives

The Strategy describes how the United States Government will enhance the security of the Air Domain while preserving the freedom of the domain for legitimate pursuits. The Strategy recognizes the critical importance of the Air Domain to the United States and the global economy, and is flexible enough to anticipate the dramatic growth in U.S. air traffic and infrastructure as well as emerging threats.

Today's terrorists have demonstrated the capability and intent to inflict a level of damage once reserved exclusively for nation-states. The nations of the world have a shared interest in maintaining and strengthening global aviation security by adopting comprehensive and cohesive policies, programs, and procedures. The Nation reserves its inherent right to self-defense and its right to act to protect its essential national security interests while protecting the United States and its interests. Defending against enemies is a fundamental responsibility of the United States Government.

In keeping with the principles from NSPD-47/HSPD-16, and consistent with the National Strategy for Combating Terrorism, that provide overarching guidance to the Strategy, and in accordance with the values enshrined in the U.S. Constitution and applicable domestic and international law, the following objectives will guide the Nation's aviation security activities:

- deter and prevent terrorist attacks and criminal or hostile acts in the Air Domain;
- protect the United States and its interests in the Air Domain;
- mitigate damage and expedite recovery;
- minimize the impact on the Aviation Transportation System and the U.S. economy; and
- actively engage domestic and international partners.

Deter and Prevent Terrorist Attacks and Criminal or Hostile Acts in the Air Domain

The United States will prevent terrorist attacks and other criminal or hostile acts in the Air Domain by maximizing shared awareness of domestic and international airspace, aviation infrastructure, and those who have access to the system. International and foreign airspace may also be of national security interest. The United States will work to: detect adversaries before they strike; deny them safe haven in which to operate unobstructed; block their freedom of movement between locations; stop them from entering the United States; identify, disrupt, and dismantle their capacities, including the capacity to possess and access weapons and financial infrastructure; use all means of attribution for maximum legal accountability including criminal prosecution; and take decisive action to eliminate the threat they pose. These actions are addressed in separate executive orders and directives and other presidential guidance.

The basis for effective prevention measures – operations and security programs – is shared awareness and sharing of risk assessment information, along with credible deterrent and interdiction capabilities. Without effective shared awareness of activities within the Air Domain, crucial opportunities for prevention or an early response can be lost. Advance warning grants time and distance to counter adversaries whether they are planning an operation or are en route to attack or to commit an unlawful act.

Effective prevention requires close cooperation between Federal, State, local, and tribal governments, the private sector, the international community, and the general public to gain shared awareness and increase security in the Air Domain while minimizing the impact of security measures on daily operations. This collaborative effort serves as a force multiplier against adversaries.

Protect the United States and its Interests in the Air Domain

Criminals and terrorists have and will continue to consider the use of the Air Domain as a means to attack the United States. The Nation must therefore continuously monitor, and exert unambiguous control over, its airspace and access to it. Security measures, combined with enhanced surveillance coverage, information collection, shared awareness, dissemination of information, and a ready response capability, will allow the United States to seize the initiative and influence events before adversaries can cause harm.

The security of the United States also depends on the security of the Aviation Transportation System's critical infrastructure, including physical and cyber networks. Complicating the security challenge is the fact that major metropolitan areas within the United States not only have airport and other Aviation Transportation System facilities, but these areas are in close proximity to other critical infrastructure such as military facilities, power plants, refineries, nuclear facilities, chemical plants, tunnels, and bridges.

Maintaining the integrity and viability of the Aviation Transportation System critical infrastructure is essential for the free movement of passengers and goods throughout the world. Some physical and cyber assets, as well as associated infrastructure, also function as defense critical infrastructure, the availability of which must be constantly assured for national security operations worldwide. Beyond the immediate casualties, the consequences of an attack on a node of critical infrastructure may include disruption of entire systems, significant damage to the economy, or the inability to deploy military forces. Protection of infrastructure networks must address individual elements, interconnecting systems, and their interdependencies.

The Department of Homeland Security is responsible for coordinating the overall national effort to enhance the protection of critical infrastructure. However, public and private sectors must work together to improve national security by: sharing threat information; conducting prudent risk assessments; working to implement essential upgrades; and investing in protective measures such as staff identification and credentialing, access control, and physical security of fixed sites.

Mitigate Damage and Expedite Recovery

The Nation must take actions to mitigate damage and expedite recovery from an attack on the Air Domain. The fundamental key to effective recovery is pre-event planning and established coordination, in conjunction with exercising national mitigation and recovery options. Mitigation and recovery actions promote resilience by preserving life, property, social, economic, and political structures, as well as restoring order and essential services for those who use the Air Domain for their livelihood. However, the Aviation Transportation System will not be shut down as an automatic response to an aviation incident; instead, the United States will be prepared to minimize the impact on the system by isolating particular portions of the Aviation Transportation System, and implementing contingency measures to ensure public safety and continuity of commerce.

The response to incidents will be in accordance with the National Response Plan (NRP), which incorporates the National Incident Management System (NIMS). The NRP provides the structure and mechanisms for national-level policy and operational coordination for domestic incident management. Pursuant to HSPD-5, the Secretary of Homeland Security serves as the principal Federal official for domestic incident management.

A terrorist attack or other disruptive incident involving the Aviation Transportation System can cause severe ripple effects on other modes of transportation as well as adverse economic or national security effects. From the onset of such an incident, Federal, State, local, and tribal governments, along with private sector entities, require the capability to assess the human and economic consequences in affected areas, and to rapidly estimate the effects on other regional, national, or global interests. These entities must also develop and implement contingency procedures to ensure continuity of operations, essential public services, and the resumption or redirection of commercial aviation activities, including the prioritized movement of cargo to mitigate the larger economic, social, and potential national security effects of the incident. For example, the public and private sectors must be ready expeditiously to: detect and identify potential WMD agents; react without endangering first responders; treat the injured; contain and minimize damage; rapidly reconstitute operations; and mitigate long-term hazards through effective decontamination measures.

Minimize the Impact on the Aviation Transportation System and the U.S. Economy

The Aviation Transportation System demands extremely high standards of security implemented in an efficient manner. Security measures should be balanced with commercial, private, and trade requirements, the safe and efficient movement of cargo and people, and economic and market competition drivers, and should protect privacy and other legal rights. To support the accelerating growth of global commerce and associated U.S. interests, security concerns and measures should, to the extent possible, be: aligned and embedded with business practices; implemented by private sector stakeholders, including air operators and related industries; optimized through the use of information technology; and implemented with the minimum essential impact on commercial and trade-flow costs and operations. The Strategy will require new and enhanced partnerships, as well as cost-sharing and burden-sharing between the public and private sectors.

To accomplish the aforementioned initiatives, the Nation must develop security measures that can be integrated with the unique needs of the aviation sector and provide a high degree of protection, while minimizing the impact to the efficient flow of people and goods through the system. The Nation must depend on new and emerging technologies to assist in this effort, such as the enhancement of biometric solutions for access control initiatives. This effort must also be supported by building and strengthening partnerships between the government and the private sector to: facilitate the continued implementation of security measures; maximize collaborative planning; and coordinate operational responses to incidents.

The effects of response and recovery efforts should also reflect aviation sector needs. On September 11, 2001, the National Airspace System was completely shut down, causing significant operational and economic impacts to the aviation sector. Recognizing the need for diverse and flexible options that allow for an effective response, the United States Government has developed plans allowing for the selective suspension or restriction of air traffic on a local or regional basis as necessary. Plans such as the Emergency Security Control of Air Traffic and other available tools and resources provide government leaders with options for the closure and the reconstitution of the system and include identifying the steps necessary to prevent the recurrence of an event. Efforts such as these will allow the government to continue to provide the security required to protect the Aviation Transportation System while minimizing the impact of those actions on the system and the U.S. economy.

Actively Engage Domestic and International Partners

Effective aviation security includes efforts at home and abroad. Active engagement among Federal, State, local, and tribal governments and private sector stakeholders during the planning process and subsequent follow-up actions is vital for success. Maintaining transparency in the planning effort and promoting dialogue will help increase the effectiveness of risk mitigation actions and reduce burdens on the private sector.

In addition to strengthening relationships among Federal, State, local, and tribal governments, the private sector, and the general public, the Nation must forge cooperative partnerships and alliances with other nations, as well as with public and private stakeholders in the international community. To foster this cooperation, a coordinated policy for United States Government aviation security activities with foreign governments, international and regional organizations, and the private sector must be achieved. Such coordination can help solicit support for improved global aviation security while furthering United States Government policies and goals. Through these domestic and international efforts, the Nation can inculcate common security measures throughout the global aviation community.

Strategic Actions

The differences in ground-based and airborne aviation security measures enacted by the nations of the world, the volume of international air traffic, and the speed of aviation operations make the Air Domain uniquely susceptible to exploitation and disruption by individuals, organizations, and states. Individuals and groups hostile to the United States have demonstrated the ability, and a continuing desire, to exploit vulnerabilities and to adapt to changes in aviation security measures to attack the Nation and its global interests.

The United States recognizes that, because of the extensive global connectivity among businesses, governments, and populations, its aviation security policies affect other nations, and that significant local and regional incidents may have global effects. Success in securing the Air Domain will not come from the United States acting alone, but through a coalition of nations maintaining a strong and united international front. The need for a strong and effective coalition is reinforced by the fact that most of the Air Domain is under no single nation's sovereignty or jurisdiction. Additionally, increased economic interdependency and globalization, made possible by air passenger and cargo transportation, underscore the need for a coordinated international approach. The United States recognizes that the vast majority of actors and activities within the Air Domain are legitimate. The security of the Air Domain can be accomplished only by employing all instruments of national power in a fully coordinated manner in concert with other nation-states.

Aviation security is best achieved by combining public and private aviation security activities on a global scale into a comprehensive and integrated effort that addresses all aviation threats. Aviation security crosses disciplines, builds upon current and future efforts, and depends on scalable, layered security to minimize single points of vulnerability. Full and complete national and international coordination, in concert with cooperative intelligence and information sharing among public and private entities, is required to protect and secure the Air Domain.

The broad principles that provide overarching guidance to the Strategy have been used to direct the development of five strategic actions, which collectively advance the strategic objectives. The Strategy recognizes that collectively these strategic actions support strategic objectives:

- maximize domain awareness;
- deploy layered security;
- promote a safe, efficient, and secure Aviation Transportation System;
- enhance international cooperation; and
- assure continuity of the Aviation Transportation System.

Domain awareness is a critical enabler for all strategic actions. Deploying layered security addresses not only prevention and protection activities, but also the integration of domestic and international security. Clearly, international cooperation is vital to enhancing the effectiveness of each of the other strategic actions.

The Strategy and appropriate supporting plans should ensure bridging toward achieving the Next Generation Air Transportation System (NGATS). NGATS provides an overall and integrated view of future operations beyond the Strategy that will integrate key transformation activities by coordinating applicable policies, procedures, research and development with participating departments and agencies from today's operations into the Aviation Transportation System of 2025.

Maximize Domain Awareness

Maximizing Air Domain awareness is critical to achieving all of the strategic objectives including deterring and preventing terrorist attacks, as well as protecting the United States and its interests in the Air Domain and mitigating the effects of an attack. Achieving shared awareness of the Air Domain is challenging and certain threats to the Air Domain are difficult to detect and interdict. The complexity of aircraft registration and ownership processes, as well as the fluid nature of these activities, offer additional challenges.

To maximize domain awareness the Nation must have the ability to integrate surveillance data, all-source intelligence, law enforcement information, and relevant open-source data from public and private sectors, including international partners. Domain awareness is heavily dependent on advanced information collection, analysis, and sharing of that information, and requires unprecedented cooperation and action among the various elements of the public and private sectors, both nationally and internationally, while adhering to laws protecting U.S. civil liberties.

To maximize domain awareness, the United States must leverage the diverse capabilities of the intelligence and law enforcement communities to collect, analyze, integrate, and disseminate timely intelligence to provide a shared awareness for United States Government agencies and international partners.

Additionally, the Nation must refine ongoing efforts to develop shared situational awareness that integrates intelligence, surveillance, reconnaissance, flight, and other aeronautical data, navigation systems, and other operational information. To ensure effective and coordinated action, access to this domain awareness information must be made available at the appropriate classification level to agencies across the U.S. Government, other local government actors, industry partners and the international community. The Nation will continue to enhance the capabilities of current information systems and develop new capabilities and procedures to locate and track aviation threats and illicit activities. Initiatives to maximize domain awareness include:

- The United States Government will maximize its capability to detect and monitor aircraft within its airspace, from large commercial aircraft to low-altitude, low-observable manned or unmanned aircraft, as well as the area contiguous to U.S. airspace and other airspace that might be of national security interest. Priority for surveillance will be given to those assets and those regions identified in specific national level documents.

- The United States Government will enhance its situational awareness through monitoring to include the combination of information sources regarding a flight (for example, airframe characteristic, onboard sensors, crew, passengers, Federal Air Marshals onboard, Federal Flight Deck Officers and domestic and foreign law enforcement).
- The United States Government will develop and encourage regulatory and private sector initiatives to enhance supply chain security practices and advance robust information collection for persons and cargo.
- The United States Government will work with international partners to develop agreements that promote enhanced visibility into the aviation supply chain and the movement of cargo and passengers and will participate in international coalitions to share aviation situational awareness, as protocols permit, on a timely basis.
- The United States Government will continue to improve and invest in an analytic work force, enhanced sensor technology, human intelligence collection, and information processing tools to persistently monitor the Air Domain.
- The United States Government will enhance the global aviation intelligence capability to strengthen intelligence analysis, coordination, and integration.
- The United States Government will enhance the Aviation Transportation System to provide shared situational awareness to disseminate information to both public and private users at the Federal, State, local, and tribal levels.
- The United States Government will support transformational research and development programs in information fusion and analysis to advance to the next level of threat assessment.
- The United States Government, with the cooperation of its foreign partners, will monitor those aircraft, cargo, and persons of interest from the point of origin, throughout the route of flight, to the point of entry, to ensure the integrity of the transit, to manage aviation traffic routing, and if necessary, to interdict and/or divert aircraft for law enforcement or defensive action.

Deploy Layered Security

Deploying layered security will be a critical enabler for strategic objectives such as deterring and preventing terrorist attacks, protecting the United States and its interests in the Air Domain, and mitigating damage and expediting recovery. The ability to achieve aviation security is contingent upon an active, layered aviation security and defense in-depth that integrates the capabilities of public and private sector entities acting in concert and using diverse and complementary measures, rather than relying on a single point solution. At a minimum, a layered approach to aviation security means further applying some measure of security to each of the following points: transportation; staff; passengers; conveyances; access control; cargo and baggage; airports; and in-flight security. Together, as one integrated system, these measures allow for resilience against expected and unexpected attack scenarios. Not only does each layer add to security, but its combination serves as a force multiplier. This layered security deters attacks, which otherwise might be executed in a multiple, simultaneous, catastrophic manner, by continually disrupting an adversary's deliberate planning process. The implementation of a new security layer must be cost effective, both in absolute terms and relative to other possible measures, and must protect information privacy and other rights provided by law. Initiatives to enhance layered security include the following:

- The United States Government will further integrate and align all aviation security programs and initiatives into a comprehensive, cohesive national effort of scalable, layered security.
- The United States Government will enhance its capabilities and procedures to identify, intercept, and defeat aviation threats in the air or on the ground.
- The United States Government will expand domestic partnerships with the public and private sector to train and equip domestic security forces, consistent with their jurisdiction and legal authority, to provide physical security for key assets and critical infrastructure to detect, identify, interdict, and defeat aviation threats on the ground.
- The United States Government will conduct and sponsor further development, and where appropriate, encourage implementation of new and emerging technologies including both aircraft-borne and ground-based systems for detection of WMD, as well as for reducing susceptibility/vulnerability or increasing survivability of aircraft to these and other terrorist threats.
- The United States Government will enhance procedures for identifying and designating flights of interest, as well as coordinating procedures for any subsequent operational response.
- The United States must have well-trained, properly equipped, and ready ground-based aviation security response forces from State, regional, local, and tribal law enforcement agencies, in addition to a Federal response force ready to detect, deter, interdict, and defeat any potential adversary.
- The United States Government will further collaborate with State, local, and tribal governments and the private sector to assess and prioritize critical facilities, resources, infrastructure, and venues that are at greatest risk from hostile or unlawful acts.
- The United States Government will enhance and expand its capability to assess risks posed by individuals with access to the Air Domain.
- The United States Government, using a risk-based methodology, will continue to develop measures for the prevention and detection of MANPADS or other stand-off weapon attack on domestic commercial aircraft.

Integrating diverse aviation security layers not only requires a clear delineation of roles and responsibilities but also a mutual understanding and acceptance of the supporting nature of overlapping authorities and capabilities of U.S. Government departments and agencies. In particular, to achieve unity of effort and operational effectiveness, aviation security assets must have a high degree of interoperability, reinforced by joint interagency and international training and exercises to ensure a high rate of readiness. Coordination protocols must define procedures for ensuring national execution of aviation security policy for specific threats or incidents.

The integrated planning and management of Federal, State, local, and tribal resources, reinforced with regular exercises, is essential for an effective response. Therefore, agencies will further coordinate training, planning, and other resources, where practical and permissible, to standardize operational concepts, develop common technology requirements, and coordinate budget planning for aviation security missions. Interagency acquisition and logistics processes must support the continuous assessment of all requirements to optimize the allocation of appropriate resources and capabilities. Cooperative research and development efforts, coupled with reformed acquisition processes with coordinated requirements, funding, and scheduling, along with management, will identify current and future needs.

Promote a Safe, Efficient, and Secure Aviation Transportation System

Promoting a safe, efficient, and secure system will help meet the strategic objectives of protecting the United States and its interests in the Air Domain and minimizing the impact on the Aviation Transportation System and the U.S. economy. Potential adversaries will attempt to exploit existing vulnerabilities, choosing the time and place to act according to the weaknesses they perceive. Private owners and operators of infrastructure, facilities, and resources are the first line of defense and should undertake basic facility security improvements. Defenses against terrorist attacks and criminal acts can be improved by embedding scalable security measures that reduce systemic or physical vulnerabilities. The elimination of vulnerabilities depends upon incorporating best practices and establishing centers of excellence, including feedback mechanisms for lessons learned, and open avenues for internal and external stakeholders to propose and develop security innovations, as well as a periodic review of each country's security standards for mutual compatibility. Initiatives to promote a safe, efficient, and secure Aviation Transportation System include the following:

- The United States Government will assume the function, currently performed by the airlines, of checking passenger information against terrorist watchlist information maintained by the United States Government and vetting such information before the departure of any regularly scheduled commercial flight for which the place of departure, the place of destination, or any scheduled stopping place is within the United States (a "U.S. Flight"). The United States Government will also determine the security utility of performing such function with respect to flights that only pass through U.S. airspace and, if necessary, develop a system by which this function will be performed for such flights.
- The United States Government will continue to collaborate with domestic and international partners to identify options to enhance risk-based screening of passengers, including, the checking of passenger information against terrorist watchlist information for regularly scheduled commercial passenger flights that overfly the territorial airspace of the United States.
- The United States Government, in coordination with public and private partners, will establish requirements for the continued implementation of air cargo transportation security measures, including all-cargo carriers, combination carriers, and indirect air carriers operating to, from, or within the United States.
- The United States Government will develop requirements for the improvement of airspace and air traffic management-related security measures.

- The United States Government and the private sector will continue to conduct vulnerability assessments to identify security measures that require improvement. A consistent risk management approach, which requires a comprehensive assessment of threat, likelihood, vulnerability, and criticality, will allow the private sector to invest in protective measures as a supporting business function.
- The United States Government will encourage the private sector, by means of outcome-based security standards, incentives, and market mechanisms, to conduct comprehensive self-assessments of its supply chain security practices.
- The United States Government will recommend measures to strengthen the prevention of entry by, and detection of, individuals with malicious intent who possess or seek to possess clearance or credentials that permit entry into secure or restricted areas within the Aviation Transportation System.

Enhance International Cooperation

Enhancing international cooperation will be a critical enabler for strategic objectives such as protecting the United States and the Air Domain, actively engaging domestic and international partners, as well as deterring and preventing terrorist attacks and criminal or hostile acts. The United States supports enhancing cooperation among nations and international organizations that share common interests regarding the security of the Air Domain. New initiatives are needed to ensure that all nations fulfill their responsibilities to prevent and respond to terrorist or criminal actions with timely and effective enforcement, including:

- The United States Government will work with foreign partners to enhance international mechanisms to improve transparency in the registration of aircraft, identification of aircraft owners, and transparency of the cargo supply chain.
- The United States Government will further cooperate with foreign partners to enhance and encourage adoption of international standards and best practices as well as to align regulation and enforcement measures. This will include initiatives pursued through international organizations, such as the International Civil Aviation Organization (ICAO), that include industry participation.
- The United States Government will enhance cooperative mechanisms for coordinating international responses to aviation threats that may span national boundaries and jurisdictions. The United States will continue to work closely with other governments and international and regional organizations to enhance the aviation security capabilities of other key nations by offering aviation and airport security assistance, training, and consultation.
- The United States Government will promote the implementation of the international anti-air piracy conventions and other international aviation security arrangements and initiatives.

Assure Continuity of the Aviation Transportation System

Assuring the continuity of the Aviation Transportation System will be a critical enabler for strategic objectives such as mitigating damage and expediting recovery, as well as minimizing the impact on the Aviation Transportation System. The United States will be prepared to maintain vital commerce and defense readiness in the aftermath of an attack or other similarly disruptive incident that may occur within the Air Domain. Threats in the Air Domain are dynamic and adaptive; therefore, prevention and protection efforts cannot be relied upon to prevent all attacks. Resiliency of the Aviation Transportation System and response and recovery efforts are important to minimize the consequences of a disruption within the system and U.S. economy. This requires: a common framework with clearly defined roles for those charged with response and recovery; ready forces that are properly trained and equipped to manage incidents, especially those involving WMD; carefully crafted and exercised contingency plans for response, recovery, and reconstitution; and extensive coordination among public, private, and international communities. Initiatives to assure the continuity of the Aviation Transportation System include:

- The United States Government will develop response and recovery protocols, consistent with the NIMS, to ensure a comprehensive and integrated national effort. Ultimately, these efforts will also need to be aligned with the National Preparedness Goal (NPG), which will establish readiness priorities, targets, and metrics.
- The United States Government will enhance the emergency preparedness for the Aviation Transportation System. This will include pre-staging of resources as necessary, coordinating, and planning exercises with first responders, and planning for restoring the function of the Aviation Transportation System in the event of an incident.
- The United States Government will develop protocols, mechanisms, and processes to mitigate the operational and economic damage from an attack, including the possibility of temporarily suspending or restricting flight operations in select areas of the National Airspace System.
- The United States Government, in coordination with public and private sector partners, will establish near-term and long-term recovery strategies to support the Aviation Transportation System in the event of an attack.
- The United States Government will identify gaps in recovery option capabilities and, working with our State, local, and tribal government, private sector, and international partners, develop appropriate operational and technical solutions to address those gaps.

The direct and indirect costs associated with a prolonged and systemic disruption of the Aviation Transportation System can be significantly reduced by following the provisions of in-place contingency and continuity plans. These plans for assessment, recovery, and reconstitution must prioritize local, regional, and national interests, as well as manage risk and uncertainty within acceptable levels. These contingency and continuity plans must be developed and exercised in a coordinated fashion by the public and private sectors.

Roles and Responsibilities

Because of the complexity and global nature of the Aviation Transportation System, responsibility for preventing, responding to, and, if necessary, recovering from attacks in the Air Domain extends across all levels of government and across private and public sectors. No single entity alone can prevent or mitigate the impact of an attack in the Air Domain.

The entities below have roles and responsibilities that fulfill executive orders or statutory responsibilities for Air Domain activities. Given the unique operating environment of the Air Domain, any of these entities may need to perform a specific lead or supporting functional role based on the threat scenario and the outcome desired by the United States Government. In determining whether a specific entity is suitable to perform this role, the following criteria will be considered:

- existing law;
- desired outcome;
- response capabilities required;
- asset availability; and
- authority to act.

To the maximum extent feasible and appropriate, Federal departments and agencies must coordinate their activities with other Federal, State, local, and tribal governments, as well as law enforcement and emergency response agencies.

Department of Homeland Security (DHS)

In accordance with NSPD-47/HSPD-16, the Secretary of Homeland Security is responsible for closely coordinating United States Government activities encompassing the national aviation security programs including identifying conflicting procedures, identifying vulnerabilities and consequences, and coordinating corresponding interagency solutions. In support of these responsibilities, the Secretary of Homeland Security:

- will conduct regular reviews of national aviation security programs to identify conflicting procedures, identify changes to threats, vulnerabilities, and resulting consequences, and coordinate corresponding interagency mitigation measures;
- will inform Federal government departments when there have been fundamentally significant recommended or actual changes resulting from regular reviews of national aviation security programs;
- will undertake additional initiatives, as appropriate, to maximize aviation security for the United States and its interests;
- is responsible for aviation security law enforcement operations and enforcement and investigation of criminal law violations within the jurisdiction of its law enforcement components;
- is responsible at borders and ports-of-entry for inspection, determining admissibility, and monitoring of persons, conveyances, and cargo traveling via air to ensure compliance with all U.S. laws, including those designed to prevent terrorists,

criminals, and terrorist weapons and contraband from entering or exiting the United States; for securing the transport of passengers and cargo by air through domestic and international screening of passengers, baggage, and air cargo; for issuing regulations and security directives necessary to ensure the security of commercial and general aviation aircraft and airport operations; for deployment of law enforcement on U.S. flagged commercial flights; and for coordination of airport access control and other security measures;

- is responsible for directing law enforcement activity related to the safety of passengers onboard aircraft that are involved in acts of hijackings and air piracy from the moment all external doors of the aircraft are closed following boarding until those doors are opened to allow passengers to leave the aircraft;
- is responsible for collaborating with State, local, and tribal governments and the private sector to assess and prioritize critical facilities, resources, infrastructure, and venues that are at greatest risk from hostile or unlawful acts;
- is responsible for developing technologies to protect assets in the Air Domain against threats such as WMD, MANPADS, and carry-on/cargo weapons (but not high-end military threats like cruise missiles, which are the purview of the Department of Defense (DoD)), and developing other technologies that facilitate protective measures such as voice and data communications with Federal law enforcement officers;
- is responsible for operational coordination with other United States Government departments and agencies, as well as with foreign governments, in the prevention of and response to aviation security incidents;
- is responsible for advancing common security interests in the Air Domain; and
- is responsible for effecting information sharing related to aviation security in support of an improved global aviation security network.

Department of Transportation (DOT)

The Secretary of Transportation, whose Department includes the country's civil aviation authority and air navigation services provider, is responsible for the regulation and operation of the National Airspace System (NAS). As an integral part of his responsibilities, the Secretary of Transportation is responsible for protecting the nation and U.S. interests in the Air Domain by conducting a broad range of national defense, homeland security, law enforcement, and crisis response related activities, including, but not limited to the following:

- the safe, efficient, and, in cooperation with the Secretaries of Homeland Security and Defense, and other key stakeholders, secure operation of aircraft flying within the country's airspace and that airspace that has been delegated to the United States for the purposes of air navigation services;
- coordinating and managing the air navigation services, regulatory activities, and related functions to support national defense, homeland security, law enforcement, and crisis response missions undertaken by Federal, State, local, and tribal entities, including the imposition of temporary flight restrictions and provision of Air Traffic Control support;
- ensuring the safety of aviation security driven modifications to U.S. registered aircraft and of other aviation security systems, which could affect civil air traffic and the country's air navigation services;

- the security of the NAS's critical infrastructure, including Air Traffic Control facilities; and
- designated leadership of NGATS/JPDO development, responsible for coordinating of Federal Aviation Administration (FAA), DHS, DoD, National Aeronautics and Space Administration, Department of Commerce, and the Office of Science and Technology Policy participation.

Department of Justice (DOJ)

The Attorney General is responsible for:
- the ground-based tactical response to resolve or defeat a hijacking, air piracy, or other terrorist threat;
- the investigation and prosecution of terrorist acts or terrorist threats by individuals or groups inside the United States, or directed at U.S. citizens or institutions abroad, where such acts are within the Federal criminal jurisdiction of the United States;
- enforcement and investigation of criminal law violations within its jurisdiction that occur in the Air Domain, and all Federal prosecutions arising from these incidents;
- coordinating the activities of other members of the law enforcement community to detect, prevent, preempt, and disrupt terrorist attacks against the United States; and
- intelligence collection, counterintelligence, and foreign intelligence sharing under guidelines established in statute and policy.

Department of Defense (DoD)

The Secretary of Defense is responsible for:
- deterring, defending against, and defeating aviation threats to the United States and its global interests;
- airborne response and resolution of nation-state threats within the Air Domain;
- the operational response to actual or potential airborne threats in U.S. airspace or the air approaches to the United States, until the threat has either been resolved or defeated;
- taking a lead or supporting role for response to aviation terrorist threats globally as part of the United States Government's active, layered defense of the Nation;
- conducting defense support of civil authorities as directed by the President of the United States or the Secretary of Defense; and
- advising Federal civilian agencies on possible technology development solutions to capability gaps and shall consider collaborative development efforts where appropriate.
- DoD is a formally designated partner in NGATS/JPDO initiative through its leadership of the Shared Situational Awareness Integrated Product Team (IPT).

Department of State (DOS)

The Secretary of State is responsible for:
- coordinating United States Government initiatives that involve foreign governments and international organizations, including regional aviation security cooperation;
- visa adjudication;

- giving foreign policy guidance on the U.S. response to actual or potential airborne threats in the air approaches to the United States if those threats are in foreign or international airspace and this is possible in the time available;
- notifying international partners of measures that may affect the exercise of rights under bilateral or multilateral aviation agreements;
- conducting global diplomatic coordination in support of aviation operational threat response, including coordination with foreign states to obtain required authorizations for operations and to facilitate United States Government assistance to operational threat response activities within the jurisdiction of those states, when requested;
- leading operational threat response public affairs activity when it is decided to take an action or refrain from an action based primarily on considerations of foreign policy, and in these cases, the Secretary of State shall also coordinate with other applicable agencies in developing public statements regarding the operational threat response activities and in relaying appropriate press guidance to agencies requesting it;
- evaluating and granting flight clearance into the United States and its territories for foreign military and government-owned aircraft along with any aircraft chartered to transport a cabinet minister or other senior foreign government official, or other official delegation intending to land in, or overfly, the U.S. and its possessions;
- enhancing multilateral nonproliferation controls on MANPADS, and other stand-off weapons systems that pose a threat to civilian and military aviation, and engaging states to seek their adherence to and implementation of those controls;
- implementing MANPADS destruction programs to reduce the global availability of these weapons and provides training and assistance to help states fulfill their MANPADS counter-proliferation obligations and combat illicit arms trade and trafficking within and across their borders; and
- administering and authorizing sanctions that could be applied to governments, entities, or individuals that engage in the proliferation of WMD, MANPADS and other stand-off weapons systems, when those activities meet the statutory and regulatory criteria.

Department of Energy (DOE)

The Secretary of Energy is responsible for:
- providing scientific and technical expertise in nuclear weapons design and specially equipped teams to conduct search, support response, and assist in recovery, and consequence management operations during any radiological or nuclear incident;
- providing radiation detection systems and associated training at foreign border crossings, airports, and seaports to detect and deter illicit trafficking in nuclear and other radioactive materials across international borders; and
- coordinating radiologically contaminated debris management associated with disposition of WMD-related materials and aircraft that may be affected by such materials or attacks.

Department of Commerce (DOC)

The Secretary of Commerce is responsible for:
- providing aviation industry and trade policy expertise in both interagency policy efforts and international negotiations;

- engaging in cooperative efforts on aviation trade issues in numerous international bodies and fora, including ICAO, the Security and Prosperity Partnership (SPP) with Canada and Mexico, the World Trade Organization (WTO), and the Asia Pacific Economic Cooperation (APEC) forum;
- providing analysis of the impact of domestic regulations and international trade agreements on the aviation industry and the broader economy;
- providing the scientific and technical expertise necessary to measure and verify that devices, equipment, and technologies meet or exceed the requirements necessary to maintain and advance the security of the Air Domain;
- providing weather forecast and analysis services integral to the operations of the Aviation Transportation System;
- providing harmonization of U.S. and international standards that are necessary for facilitation of aviation-related commerce; and
- participating in the NGATS initiative through its leadership of the Weather IPT.

Office of The Director of National Intelligence (ODNI)

The Director of National Intelligence is responsible for:
- developing, sustaining, and continually strengthening a unified Intelligence Community enterprise that supports Federal, State, regional, local, tribal, and private sector entities by collecting, analyzing, and disseminating accurate, timely, and relevant all-source intelligence for the safe and effective use of the air, related transportation, and other threat domains;
- defining, creating, and propagating the business rules, policies, and technical standards for an Intelligence Community enterprise environment for information sharing and intelligence integration across the air related transportation, and other threat domains;
- overseeing the primary organization in the U.S. Government for analyzing and integrating all intelligence possessed or acquired by the United States Government pertaining to terrorism and counterterrorism, except intelligence pertaining exclusively to domestic terrorists and domestic counterterrorism; and
- overseeing National Intelligence Program activities that support transportation security, including in the Air Domain, by leveraging innovative collection and analytical techniques, developing and employing effective counterintelligence measures that preserve the integrity of aviation security information, and respecting the civil liberties and privacy of all Americans.

State, Local, and Tribal Governments

Some of the Nation's aviation infrastructure is owned and operated by State, local, and tribal governments. State Governors and/or homeland security agencies, in addition to local and tribal governments, hold a leadership position to address specific aviation security needs or issues and response. During extraordinary circumstances, the Federal government may assume lead security responsibility. Typically, except for cross-border traffic, lead responsibility will remain with the States, localities, or tribes. Specific responsibilities of State, local, and tribal governments are discussed in the NIPP and corresponding TSSP. State, local, and tribal governments are currently working with the Federal government to identify critical transportation assets, conduct the necessary vulnerability assessments, and develop security plans to protect those assets. They are also developing their response and recovery capabilities to address terrorist attacks and other disruptive incidents, and to meet the NPG.

Private Sector

Substantial segments of the Nation's aviation transportation infrastructure are owned and operated by private sector entities. As such, an effective national aviation security strategy must be supported by a private sector that internalizes a strong security culture, embedding best practices and government requirements into day-to-day operations. It is the responsibility of private sector owners to conduct and execute business continuity planning, integrate security planning with disaster recovery planning, and to actively participate with Federal, State, local, and tribal governments to improve security in the aviation sector.

Conclusion

The Strategy presents a vision for aviation security that seeks to secure the people and interests of the United States. Moreover, it underscores the Nation's commitment to strengthening international partnerships and advancing economic well-being around the globe by facilitating commerce and abiding by the principles of freedom of the airways. The sheer magnitude of the Air Domain complicates the arduous and complex task of maintaining aviation security. The United States confronts a diverse set of adversaries fully prepared to exploit this vast domain for nefarious purposes. The Air Domain serves as the medium for a variety of threats that honor no national frontier and that seek to imperil the peace and prosperity of the world. Many of these threats mingle with legitimate commerce, either to provide concealment for carrying out hostile acts, or to make available weapons of mass destruction, their delivery systems, and related materials to nations and non-state actors of concern.

In this ambiguous security environment, responding to these unpredictable threats requires teamwork to prevent attacks, protect people and infrastructure, minimize damage, and expedite recovery. The response necessitates the integration and alignment of all aviation security programs and initiatives into a far-reaching and unified national effort involving Federal, State, local, and tribal governments, as well as private sector organizations. Since September 11, 2001, Federal departments and agencies have risen uncompromisingly to the challenge of ensuring aviation security. The challenges that remain ahead for the Nation, the adversaries it confronts, and the environment in which it operates compel the United States to strengthen its ties with international partners and to seek new relationships with others. Therefore, international cooperation is critical to ensuring that lawful private and public activities in the Air Domain are protected from attack and hostile or unlawful exploitation. Such collaboration is fundamental to worldwide economic stability and growth, and it is vital to the interests of the United States. It is only through such an integrated approach among all aviation partners, governmental and non-governmental, public, and private, that the United States can improve the security of the Air Domain.

Thus, effective implementation of the Strategy requires greater cooperation. It requires deeper trust and confidence, not less. It requires a concerted application of collective capabilities to: increase awareness of all people, activities, and events in the Air Domain; enhance aviation security frameworks domestically and internationally through constant innovation; deploy an active, layered aviation security and defense in-depth based on law enforcement authorities, military capabilities, and private sector partners' competencies; pursue transformational research and development to move to the next level of information fusion and analysis and WMD detection technologies for qualitative improvements in threat detection; improve our response posture should a threat emerge; and enhance our recovery should an incident occur.